Can I Tell You About...

Being a Young Carer?

CAN I TELL YOU ABOUT...?

The "Can I tell you about...?" series offers simple introductions to a range of conditions, issues and big ideas that affect our lives. Friendly characters invite readers to learn about their experiences, share their knowledge and teach us to empathise with others. These books serve as excellent starting points for family and classroom discussions.

Other subjects covered in the Can I tell you about...? series

Can I Tell You About...

Being a Young Carer?

A Guide for Children, Family and Professionals

Jo Aldridge
Illustrated by Jack Aldridge Deacon

Jessica Kingsley *Publishers*
London and Philadelphia

First published in 2019
by Jessica Kingsley Publishers
73 Collier Street
London N1 9BE, UK
and
400 Market Street, Suite 400
Philadelphia, PA 19106, USA

www.jkp.com

Library of Congress Cataloging in Publication Data
Names: Aldridge, Jo, author.
Title: Can I tell you about being a young carer? : a guide for friends,
family and professionals / Jo Aldridge.
Description: London ; Philadelphia : Jessica Kingsley Publishers, 2019.
Identifiers: LCCN 2018024749 | ISBN 9781785925269
Subjects: LCSH: Child caregivers--Great Britain--Juvenile literature. |
Children of parents with disabilities--
Great Britain--Juvenile literature.
| Caregivers--Great Britain--Juvenile literature.
Classification: LCC HQ759.67 .A429 2019 | DDC
362/.04250941--dc23 LC record available at https://catalog.
loc.gov/vwebv/searchBrowse?editSearchId=E

British Library Cataloguing in Publication Data
A CIP catalogue record for this book is available from the British Library

ISBN 978 1 78592 526 9
eISBN 978 1 78450 922 4

Printed and bound in the United States

Manufactured by Thomson-Shore, Dexter, MI (USA); RMA27NS166, November, 2018

CONTENTS

ACKNOWLEDGEMENTS

With grateful thanks to all of the children and families with whom I have worked over the years, including carers young and older. Thank you also to Daniel Phelps at the University of Winchester for his very helpful review of an early draft of the book. Thanks must go also to the excellent team at JKP, specifically Elen Griffiths and Sean Townsend.

INTRODUCTION

In some families, children help to care for a relative (parent, brother or sister or grandparent) who is ill or disabled or who has problems with alcohol or drugs. When children care for a relative who faces these problems they are often called "young carers", although some children may not even know or realise that they are carers or describe themselves as a young carer.

A young carer may provide lots of care in the home for their relative or they might just be helping out every so often – all families are different and each young carer will have a different family and caring experience. But the kinds of things young carers do when they care are often very similar. For example, they might be helping to cook or clean in the house because their relative is unable to do this, or they might be helping to look after a brother or sister when their mum or dad is ill.

Being a young carer can be difficult for some children, for others it can be a positive experience. *Can I Tell You About Being a Young Carer?* is a guide for children who are carers or who think they might be a young carer. It explains the kinds of things young carers do, the way this makes children feel and the sorts of things that young carers need.

Can I Tell You About Being a Young Carer? is also a guide for families, friends and professionals, such as teachers and teaching assistants, who want to know more about what it is like being a young carer and what they can do to help. Some children want to care, while others do not, and there are lots of things that families, friends and professionals can do to lend their support. Some young carers have said that one person, such as a teacher or a social worker, can make a big difference to their lives just by listening to them and understanding their situation.

Extra information is included at the back of this book to help family, friends and professionals understand how they can best support children who are carers, and to help them live the life they want to lead.

"Hello. My name is Carly and I am 12. I live with my mum, my little brother Sam, who is five, and my dog Scruff. My dad doesn't live with us.

I am a young carer and I help to look after my mum who has multiple sclerosis, which means the muscles in her arms and legs don't work properly. Mum also has depression, which means she gets sad a lot.

Because of my mum's illness she has to use a wheelchair and on bad days she is often too tired and sad to get out of bed, so some days she stays there all day. On these days I am in charge and I do lots of things around the house and to help my little brother.

On my mum's good days when she is feeling happier, we go out to the shops together and for walks with Sam and Scruff, and we laugh and joke all the time."

"When Mum is not feeling well and is sad I try to cheer her up by helping around the house, playing with Sam and telling her jokes and stories to try and make her laugh. On Mum's really bad days I do the cooking too – nothing fancy or difficult, just things like making beans on toast or soup and sandwiches. I also sometimes have to help her wash and go to the toilet when she is really finding it hard to move.

I clean up around the house when Mum can't, and most mornings I get Sam ready for school and take Scruff out for walks. I love walking Scruff but I don't always like doing the other stuff around the house, like cleaning and putting the washing in the machine, because it takes ages and it means I don't have much time to spend doing the things I like to do, like playing with Scruff and watching TV.

Someone called a social worker (she's called Barbara) came to the house to speak to Mum and me about what Mum needs because she is ill and in a wheelchair. It was Barbara who told me that because of the sorts of things I do in the house and for Sam this is called being a 'young carer'. She said there are lots of other children like me who do the same and other kinds of things when their parents are ill. This made me feel a bit better – not so alone with it all."

"Because Mum has multiple sclerosis (it's usually just called 'MS') and also because of her depression and the fact she's on her own, this means she can't always look after me and Sam in the way that other parents do who aren't ill. That's why I have to look after us all sometimes.

I know my mum doesn't like the fact that I have to care for her, and for Sam too sometimes. It makes her more sad and upset when she sees me doing things in the house she thinks she should be doing. But some days she just isn't up to it and also there isn't always anyone else around who can do these kinds of things – not all the time like me. And we don't have any other relatives or friends who live near us.

Our social worker, Barbara, is trying to get more help for us so I don't have to do so much, like someone to come in and help Mum around the house, do the cleaning and stuff and get Sam ready for school, but this hasn't happened yet. Barbara says it's sometimes the same for other children like me whose mum or dad is ill."

"Sometimes I get a bit upset because I have to do so much in the house and for Mum and Sam. It means that I don't always get to do the things I want to do and I can't always go out with my friends because I don't want to leave Mum or Sam on their own.

It's hard getting Sam ready for school in the morning sometimes, as well as having to get myself ready and check that Mum is all right. On her good mornings she can get our breakfasts and get Sam ready, but if she isn't feeling well then she is sometimes still in bed when I go to school. I know on those days too I will have to go to the shops and get us all something to eat when I get back from school – I don't really like doing all that because it means I might not have enough time to do my homework. But I can't go to the homework club at school either because I have to get home for Mum and Sam.

Sometimes Mum forgets to take her tablets or is asleep and I have to remind her to take them. I don't like having to do this because she has a lot of tablets to take and I'm worried that I might forget too.

Holidays are easier because I am at home more and I can spend time with Mum and Sam, and Scruff. It also means I get time to spend doing the kinds of things I like. At the moment I'm writing and drawing a life story book about our family life. I love doing things like that."

"Sometimes I worry about Mum and what might happen to her. I know that MS is quite serious and she has got worse, in that she didn't always use her wheelchair, but she uses it pretty much all the time now.

Barbara, our social worker, has talked to me about this and tried to explain it, but there's still stuff I don't understand. Like, will Mum just end up being in bed all the time? Will she have to go into hospital? What will happen to me and Sam if she does?

I don't know if there is a cure either for MS or for depression. I went with Mum once to the doctor's so I could try and understand more about her illnesses, but I just ended up getting more confused because the doctor used long words that I didn't understand and she didn't really speak to me at all.

Sometimes I worry about Mum when I'm at school too. I wonder how she is at home on her own and then I don't always pay enough attention in class. I got told off for this one time by my teacher in a maths lesson. I wanted to explain to Mr Carter but didn't in the end as I didn't really know what to say and got all tongue-tied when he asked me in front of the class if there was anything wrong."

"I don't always tell others either about Mum and about what I do to help her and Sam around the house. My best friend Hannah knows because she lives just down the road and she's been to my house. And because I trust her and know she won't tell anyone else if I don't want her to. It's not that it's a secret, it's just that I know our family isn't like other families and sometimes I worry what will happen if, say, I told someone I was a young carer.

On Mum's good days I feel really close to her, and I'm glad that I help to look after her. But sometimes, when she's sad and cries a lot, I don't know how to help her and I feel angry with myself. Sometimes I feel angry with her too even though I know it's not her fault, and then I end up feeling guilty.

I have just started going to a young carers project in town. I really like it. It's a club for kids like me whose parents are ill, or sometimes it's a brother or sister or grandparent. I've made a friend there called Dean. He's my age and he helps his mum to look after his granddad who lives in their house with them. He is really ill and forgets things all the time and keeps falling over. Dean has to make sure he's safe, make him drinks and stay with him when his mum goes out.

Dean and I talk about our families and what it's like caring for someone like your mum or granddad. I feel like he really understands because we are both in the same situation. We are both 'young carers'. The two people who run the young carers project, Mark and Aisha, are really friendly and organise trips to the cinema and homework clubs for us. They also make sure Mum and Sam are okay when we come to the project."

"I love being with my family, my mum and Sam and Scruff. Even when Mum is having a bad day and is difficult to talk to or get through to, I still love her to bits; and a lot of the time it makes me feel good about myself when I help out with Sam and around the house – I've learnt a lot of things about cooking and looking after the house that my friends wouldn't understand at all. I know that doing these things, even though they can be difficult sometimes, is actually helping Mum. I hope that it might help her get better too, make her feel a bit happier when she's sad and upset.

It has really helped me going to the young carers project, even though I haven't been going for very long. Going there and talking to Dean and the other friends I've made at the project, as well as to Mark and Aisha, has helped me deal with caring a lot better. We don't always talk about home or caring but we support each other when we need to. It has also made me realise that I don't have to care on my own, that I can get help so that I don't have to take it all on myself.

I think it's also helped me, Mum and Sam get on much better because now I understand much more about how hard it is for families like ours when a parent is ill for a long time or has a disability that means they can't always do the stuff they want to around the house, and for their children.

I have also started thinking about what I want to do when I leave school, and Mark and Aisha have helped me see that it's okay to do things that I enjoy doing and to make plans even though Mum is poorly. I would really love to be a vet. I already know a lot about dogs and how to look after them properly because I look after Scruff all the time, take him out for walks, feed him and make sure he's healthy and happy. He makes us all laugh sometimes, especially with the daft things he does like going round and round in crazy circles chasing his tail."

“I don't get a lot of time to myself, what with making sure Mum and Sam are okay and school and everything. But if I'm feeling down or upset about something I take Scruff out for a walk to take my mind off things – sometimes it's good to get out of the house even for a little while. I know it's important also to do things that I enjoy and to have fun and not always worry about what's going on at home.

Other times I know I need to talk to someone about what I'm going through – about what it's like helping to look after Mum and Sam and being in charge of everything (that's what it feels like sometimes). I can talk to Mum but I don't always want to bother her with how I'm feeling, and sometimes I worry about her and don't want to tell her that's what's bothering me. So then it's good to talk to someone else. Dean understands because he knows what it's like being a young carer. Aisha and Mark are really good too – I can talk to them about anything and that really helps knowing they are there.

They've also said it might be a good idea to talk to one of my teachers about what it's like for me at home and what I have to do around the house and for Sam. They can help me do that, so I am thinking about it because I think if school know then they might be able to help me and understand more when I can't always hand my homework in on time.

Aisha and Mark have also given me lots of information about where I can go for support and the kinds of places and websites where we can all ask for help (me, Mum and Sam). This has made me feel a lot better about things because it means I don't feel so alone or worried about having to cope on my own with everything."

"Talking about being a young carer helps me but that's not who or what I am all the time. Other people need to understand that I am more than a young carer – I am a child, a daughter to Mum, a sister to Sam, and someone who's good at a lot of things like writing, maths (at school) and dog walking!

I love my mum and my family and I don't want anything to change that – I don't want the fact that I sometimes have to care for Mum and Sam to mean that others think I can't cope. I can cope but I need help and support to help me live my life like other children whose parents aren't ill or disabled.

It is sometimes difficult to talk about my family and my mum's illness and her disability to others who I don't know well or who I don't trust. That means that I don't always tell people that I am a young carer. If I do tell someone though I really don't want them to feel sorry for me or to tell me what to do. I want someone to ask me how I'm doing, and to say that they understand and that they can help me, and my family, if I want them to.

I need those people who could help me, such as my teachers, to try to understand what it is like to be a young carer and to give me the right kind of information and support that will be best for me and my family. The kind of support I would like is to be able to go to after-school clubs without worrying about how Mum and Sam will cope without me. It would also really help me if school teachers were more understanding about the fact that I can't always get my homework in on time.

I really want to be a vet when I leave school. I know that will mean going to college and also maybe even going away to university. I need help understanding how I will be able to do this without leaving Mum on her own all the time or Sam to care for her on his own. Whatever happens I need for them to be safe and happy, and I want the same for me too."

USEFUL RESOURCES, ORGANISATIONS AND WEBSITES

There are a number of resources available for young carers and their families and for the people who support them, such as teachers and social workers. Some of these are written for children and young people, and others are for adults who help young carers and their families. The main ones are listed below.

FOR CHILDREN AND FAMILIES

Carers Trust is a national charitable organisation that provides information about and for young carers and their families, including advice about young carers' and young adult carers' rights, health and wellbeing, and advice about where to get support and how to find local services. Visit their website at: https://carers.org/about-us/about-young-carers. Carers Trust have also produced a short video about a young carer: *Pie – A Story for Young Carers* describes the determination of one young carer to look after his granny in the same way that she used to look after him (www.youtube.com/watch?v=bGyytZkwK88).

The Children's Society is a national charity that provides information and support for young carers and their families. Every year The Children's Society also puts on a national Young Carers Festival which aims to recognise, inform and consult with young carers so that their needs and those of their families can be met in better ways. You can read more about their work, including the range of resources they offer, the Young Carers Festival and a video about young caring (*Molly's Story*) here: www.childrenssociety.org.uk/what-we-do/helping-children/supporting-young-carers

Barnardo's (a national children's charity) provides support services for young carers across the UK. Their website gives details about these services and provides a range of information and resources for young carers and their families: www.barnardos.org.uk/what_we_do/our_work/ young_carers.htm

Here you can also watch four videos of children and young people talking about caring as well as a video of the Indigo Project, which supports young carers by giving them a break from caring.

The *NHS Choices* website (www.nhs.uk/conditions/ social-care-and-support/young-carers-rights) also provides information for children and young people who are carers, including contact details for the *Carers Direct Helpline* (0300 123 1053).

Children and young people aged 16 to 24 who are caring are sometimes called "young adult carers". Many of the organisations above also provide information and advice for young adult carers, but a dedicated source of information and advice is the *Learning and Work Institute* (LWI). This organisation prioritises the rights of young adult carers to take part in learning and to be able to access services and job opportunities. It also recognises how education providers and policy makers need to support young adult carers in order to maximise their learning and work opportunities. For further information visit the LWI website: www.learningandwork.org.uk/our-work/life-and-society/citizens-curriculum/young-adult-carers

There are currently around 250 young carers projects across the UK that provide support to young carers in local areas. This support includes young carers clubs – including homework clubs – and leisure and respite activities (giving children and young people a break from caring). You will be able to find out if there is a young carers project in your area either by doing a Google search that includes the name of your city or county and putting "young carers project" after the name; or you can go on your city or county council's website and type "support for young carers" in the "search" box on the website. All local authorities should provide information about the support they offer to young carers, including how to request a young carer's needs assessment. Here is an example of the kind of information local authorities provide (from Nottinghamshire County Council): www.nottinghamshire.gov.uk/care/adult-social-care/carers/support-for-young-carers

Childline (www.childline.org.uk/info-advice/home-families/family-relationships/young-carers) also offers support to young carers, including a range of information about where to go to ask for help and their free telephone helpline number: 0800 1111.

FOR PROFESSIONALS

The following organisations and websites provide a range of resources to professionals, including teachers and children's and adult social care workers who support young carers (including young adult carers) and their families:

Social Care Institute for Excellence (SCIE): www.scie.org.uk/atoz/?f_az_subject_thesaurus_terms_s=young+carers&st=atoz

SCIE provides resources and information about duties and provisions under the Care Act 2014.

Carers Trust and *The Children's Society* also provide additional resources for professionals who support young carers and their families, including dedicated resources for supporting young carers in schools and (for young adult carers) in further and higher education, employment and training:

Carers Trust: https://professionals.carers.org

See also: https://professionals.carers.org/young-carers-and-school

https://youngcarersinschools.com

https://carerspassports.uk/education/schools

The Children's Society: www.childrenssociety.org.uk/youngcarer/resources-for-professionals

Both the Care Act 2014 and the Children and Families Act 2014 include requirements for local authorities' professionals to identify and support young carers and young adult carers and their families. Carers Trust and The Children's Society provide resources for professionals about these requirements and how to implement needs assessments for young carers and their families (see their websites listed on the previous page).

Research in Practice (RiP) promotes evidence-based practice in children's services, and aims to address the gaps between research, practice and service users' experiences in order to improve professional practice and transform the lives of children and families. RiP has produced a practice tool and guide (*Young Carers and their Families: Confident Assessment Practice*, 2016) to help children's and adult social care professionals assess the needs of young carers and their families effectively: www.rip.org.uk/resources/publications/practice-tools-and-guides/young-carers-and-their-families-confident-assessment-practice-2016

The *Association of Directors of Children's Services* (ADCS) has produced a model local Memorandum of Understanding with the Association of Directors of Adult Social Services in order to support young carers and their families: *No Wrong Doors: Working Together to Support Young Carers and their Families.* See: http://adcs.org.uk/early-help/article/no-wrong-doors-working-together-to-support-young-carers-and-their-families

Family Action have also produced a report and recommendations for teachers and other professionals who support young carers in schools: *Be Bothered: Making Education Count for Young Carers* (2012): www.family-action.org.uk/content/uploads/2014/06/Be-Bothered-Make-Education-Count-for-Young-Carers.pdf

For research evidence and information about young carers and their families visit the *Young Carers Research Group* website (Loughborough University, UK): www.ycrg.org.uk

For information about policy and practice on young carers, including young adult and student carers, see: www.youngcarers.info (this website is run by Daniel Phelps at the University of Winchester).